Sweetened Condensed
Poetry & Photographs

by Rebecca Grabill

Flying Ketchup Press
Kansas City, MO

Special thank you to FountainVerse Poetry Festival Kansas City
which inspired this publication.

Flying Ketchup Press® is a trademarked small press seeking submissions through
Submittable.com to discover and develop new voices in poetry, drama, fiction and
non-fiction with a special emphasis in new short stories. We are a publisher made
by and for creatives in the Heartland. Our dream is to salvage lost treasure troves of
written and illustrated work-- to create worlds of wonder and delight; to share stories.
Maybe yours.
Find us at www.flyingketchuppress.com

All inquiries should be addressed to:
Flying Ketchup Press®
11608 N. Charlotte Street, Kansas City, MO 64115.

Library of Congress Cataloging-Publication Data

Grabill, Rebecca

Library of Congress Control Number: 2019912935

ISBN-13: 978-1-970151-19-0

Dedication

for Stephen

Editor's Note

Dear Gentle Reader,

Here, in these pages, you will find the journey of an author. We all start somewhere— as kids riding tricycles, as teens buying fast food. But only later can we see the enormous size and weight of all we carry with us, firmly pressed under the soles of our feet, or hidden away in an old attic. Rebecca Grabill is someone who unpacks those boxes for us: some gently and some with a kick. She dusts off each thing of value and serves it up with a wry laugh and a devil-may-care smile. It's all just fun and games until your heart skips a beat and you feel a tightness in the back of your throat, and a tear runs down your cheek.

I remember when I first met Rebecca at Hamline University's MFA program for writing for kids and young adults in St. Paul, MN. She read a first-person narrative from the voice of a young girl that about put my heart in shreds. I leaned over and whispered, "Where did you get all that? How did you write something so, so…." as I stumbled for words, she didn't. "I googled it," she joked quickly and walked away. It took me a couple of beats, and she was gone before it sunk in. As a writer, she could harness her own experiences and others and synthesize a character who seemed more familiar and truer than your own face in the mirror. I've been a fan ever since.

When I asked her to submit a manuscript for the FountainVerse Poetry Festival in Kansas City, I didn't know what I would get. Vampires, Werewolves, or something about raising chickens out in the beautiful countryside. I got nothing of the sort, just the truth, carefully unwrapped. And for that, I am thankful.

I look forward to everything Rebecca writes, and each time I'm encouraged to just let go, pick up my pen, and find a way to make my words both sweetened and condensed. Enjoy.

Polly Alice McCann

Random Words of Acknowledgment

Herein lies an amalgamation of foreword and acknowledgments, a pompous statement of the deepest meaning of this collection, the universe, and everything else. The truth? There is no deep meaning. "Of making many books there is no end," but in the making of them, truth, beauty, meaning can be discovered. These poems are sweetened—because my life, like most, has had some very bleak corners, too bleak for this collection—and it's condensed—because how do you fit forty-some-odd years into a few pages? It's a glimpse into the product, the blood, the sap, of the life of a mother, daughter, wife, writer.

More than anyone I have Polly McCann, my editor at Flying Ketchup Press, to thank. She had the vision to encourage me to assemble a collection, she pushed for "just a little more of you," and commented so aptly on an early draft that I was holding the reader at "arm's length." So come in for an embrace! (And if you can smell the baby-spit on my shirt, it's Polly's fault.)

Perhaps sharing the blame are those mentors and classmates who read and inspired a few of these poems, most notably Mary Logue whose guidance is keenly felt even today, as well as Kelly Easton (see, I sprinkled!), Phyllis Root, and Jane Resh Thomas.

I must also thank my children: those who can speak kindly gave consent for the images of themselves, and those who can't … well, don't all babies look basically the same? More seriously, they are my primary inspiration, blessing, frustration, exhaustion all at once. As I write this, a Minecraft horse neighs behind me, and some theme song plays, perhaps My Little Pony? The shower runs, two teens and a toddler sleep, and my husband leans against the kitchen counter sipping freshly made coffee, a cup of which he just delivered to my corner of the living room.

I could say something sentimental about my husband—his unwavering support—but I wrote a poem about him and he shows up in several others. Let those words speak as they will.

I hope every reader will find a little something of themselves here, perhaps a new awareness or a moment of recognition or remembrance.

Table of Contents

[Ingredients]

Tousled, 2018

Sweetened Condensed Milk

I have to stop and count
like the lollygaggers, rubberneckers
who ask if they are all mine and do I know
where babies come from, am I
done yet? I tell them,
I'm stuck in the groove
of a vintage record and crammed
into a tiny can
of paper pulp pages,
which are recycled, I swear
to god. They're reused
like the tissue in my pocket
for six small noses, to
squeeze meaning out
like milk from a ravaged nipple
in infinitesimal drops
so delicious on the tongue
like motherhood itself, over and over
and over and over
and over
and
over again—

just think about my jugs
(no, really, do)
and wonder with me …

I could have filled
the world
with all that milk.

Sunday Morning

Best way to start a new notebook,
by beginning a sonnet and scratching it out.
It was going to be a whiney thing about parenting
six children, about babies and teens
and church homilies of abstractions
into the ether of the ornate lights in the vaulted ceiling,
the ones I look to while wrestling my angel,
flashing breast to those behind us when baby pops off
a moment to squawk indignantly
at the silence of prayer.

In the poem I'm writing,
in my mind, I plan a segue into turkey sex
and that bird's general lack
of maternal instinct
and coordination.
If its eggs are fertilized (however unlikely),
very few are nurtured, like
my own child self,
or the hamster
I had as a girl, whose litter—six pups,
I think—after a week was down to four
and a half.

Hamsters don't come from eggs, of course,
unlike, say, dinosaurs.
We've evolved.
We make love like poets
and make babies
who end up wriggling
beside us in the pew
so we couldn't write a sonnet
even if we wanted to.

Sonnet of Remembrance

*I*t rises up behind my sternum first
a pocket holding thistles, thorn and some
small shred of light, a blight, unsated thirst
vampiric longing, meaning, search for home
but I'm a stranger here and everywhere,
a noxious weed that ought be pulled and cast
into the fire and then I'd be just air
and rattling bones of tears, the winter's last
sad leaves. They harbor shoots of spring, bright spikes
of green, alive and waiting, ripe, but I
am blinded by a pain behind my eyes
a tightness at my nape, the constant sigh
of breath, like spring's first breeze that tries to dry
my cheeks still damp as years turn into weeks.

Following, 2007

day in the life of a non-working mother

up at eight am Marie, the nanny, has already
roused the children, lined them up
by the door, I kiss them before
waving them out to the bus

       alarm screams 6:15
I roll over and snooze but after five
of my seven minutes
I give up, the shower rumbles

my husband has awakened the teens and poured
my tea, we discuss the state of affairs
with the laundry, the dinner plan
and just as we are at last awake enough to

       crap 7:20 have a good day
kisses goodbye to son, son, husband
I nuke tepid coffee
balance a nursing baby

while the four-year-old does his school bus prep
shoes, illogical mittens, pleading
       my pleading, not his
for one last bite of cereal as we
run down the long drive until

the bus doors sigh closed and I walk indirectly
toward the house, blissfully alone
for the briefest moment
       I inhale dewy patchouli tinged with fall
remembering mornings so long and free I can
greet the first grader with a smile

and offer her sliced strawberries
while we work on math because everything
even math
        if three kids go to school and three stay home …
especially math
is better with strawberries

my barely-teen blinks from behind sleep-tousled hair
and yawns up to the shower while baby
first grader and I color pictures
        Cat Sat on Mat, Cat Sat on Cop
her bubbling laughter carries me through

grammar and algebra with fresh-washed teen,
nursing with baby, and ten thousand first-grader pleas
for iPadNetflixIceCreamPaintsPopcorn
        nonononononojustgooutside

until I'm sprinting to the end
of the driveway where the bus driver
asks if I can hear him when he honks
my bleary just-waking preschooler trudges

toward small round pizzas, tortilla chips,
other foods I pretend are healthy
I read a novel aloud, nurse baby again
and finally, finally with baby in bed, laptop open

Marie returns to urge Do your math, darlings
Practice Hiragana, Read to your brother, Get out
of the refrigerator
until we're all sick
of one another's company

What Carries Him Away, 2019

we retreat to iPads
favorite shows for the blink of an hour
before Dad and teens come home

dinner, evening jobs, laundry, dishes, homework
husband and I attempt to share
the fading tick of daylight while baby
tosses cereal from his tray

by the handful on his way to bath
and bed I take my time nursing
in silence

reluctantly I rejoin husband, teens
X Files, Star Trek, precious wine

at last, bed, sweet bed, I'm
unconscious before I can hear
the teens turn up the TV, I drift
like the feather-laden craft

on the refrigerator, the pile of papers
waiting to be signed, the flower
plucked by tiny hands and presented
still adorned with a crawling wasp

into dreams of boarding school
for me

If

*I*f I am the fiction I've written for myself
then I want to trade my ginger for brunette,
be tan and without freckles or sensitivity
to the sun. I'll be twenty-three, two perky
eyes with perfect vision, and I'll learn Russian.

Be a spy, like I dreamed when I was
twelve. I wanted to embrace danger,
master fear that shadowed me like a cruel
twin, plotting to drop insects in my hair,
I'd never allow anyone to know my secrets.

I would live in ages long, long past,
wooed by Mr. Heathcliff on the purple
moors. I would be my alter-ego, Anne
spelled with an e. I would read
the most wonderful books
to you, my children.

I would tell you …
you are not so alone,
not so strange as you fear, not so afraid
as you could be.

I would show you worlds made of words.
I would give you a way to grow up
that I can only
imagine.

Writing is the Channeling of Childhood's Ghosts

In homage to "Poetry is the Art of Not Succeeding" by Joe Salerno

Writing is the channeling of childhood's ghosts;
the art of catching little moments
of sunshine painting a thin spectrum
on the dark closet floor, of breathing
the fragrance of dust and mothballs.

It's watching grandma turning
an old fur coat into a stuffed bear
that keeps you awake at night,
shivering under the covers, certain
that its gaze captures your breaths.

Wonderful arrays of insults; your classmates
are masters, smiths of words sharpened
by their own angry fathers. The view
out the classroom window—a swing
pushed by invisible hands.

It's moments of weaving dandelions
into fragile crowns, of milking
their stems for the last drops of summer's
blood before your lungs shrink
with a rattling winter cough.

It's finding you've been to this
place before, on a day you remember
now as warm, moist, silent except
for a whisper that you better not tell
anyone, if you know what's good for you.

Xmas List

Secret Sister: scarf
Ornament
Coffee (local)

Steve: wallet

Nicholas: stuff for dorm
Pajamas
TJ Maxx gift card (birthday)
Stocking stuffer–socks

Baz: Airsoft gear
Gas mask (birthday)
Footie pajamas
Stocking stuffer–socks

Maggie: Copic pens
Watercolor paper
Hiragana book
Earrings
Stocking stuffer—hair ties

Penny: dollhouse
Paints for dollhouse
Wallpaper for dollhouse
American Girl doll clothes
Footie pajamas
Stocking stuffer–barrettes

Kilian: Trains
School bus
Stocking stuffer—cars

Emeric: Taggie blanket
Stacking cups (birthday)

Me: socks
Knitting needles
Vodka (gluten free)

Why I Don't Watch Television

The dentin contains these
channels, blocking the pain,
providing this soothing
relief. That's why doctors
recommend—so that's
why my color stays luminous
like—our twenty dollar
dinner for two, only at—
smart shopping is what's
going on, first is—live
video chat on the go—
call on me brother when
you want—a paper towel—
switching to Chevrolet
get zero percent APR—on
art projects in the—kitchen
three times cleaner than a
dishcloth—texting can be
expensive, it all starts—tonight
at eleven on News—how
do I know my anti-aging
make-up really works?
—Tell your doctor
if you are pregnant.

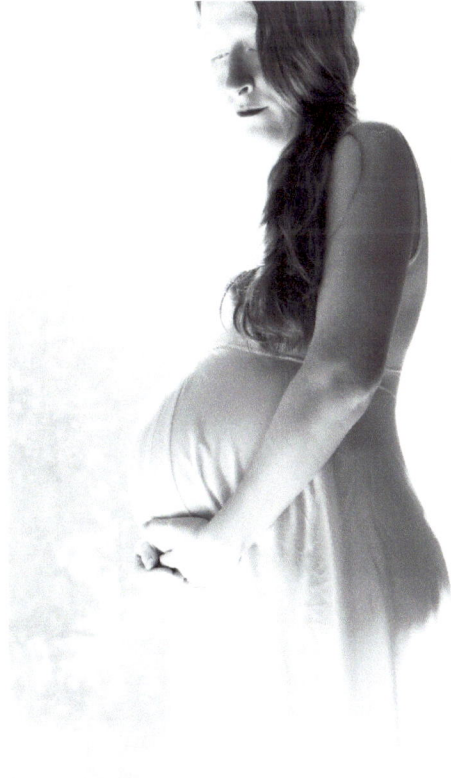

Portrait of Expectation, 2014

What Does it Mean, Unwanted?

I already have so many.
I didn't want you.
I have so many.
But not you. I never had
you. Until now.
Now every thought
spins around your axis.
Downy fluff of hair … I can't stop
            inhaling
warmth, sweet washed soap,
the distant memory of sleep.
Your tiny pulse in the fragile shallowness.
Petal ears, fingernails no larger
than a raindrop, each breath
a puff of moments on my chest.

How could I have greeted
those two pink lines
with such terror?

Beloved, 2017

Speeding Through the Country in Winter

Outside the window
blue dusk plays behind an age-chapped barn,
pale peach sunlight dusts
the snow on each leaning fence post, tops them
with a dollop of cream,
fresh skimmed.

We whir by
only glimpsing
the curved pasture,
as pale
and rose-hued
as our infant daughter's cheek.

Portrait of You (for Emeric)

If I could capture your likeness, I'd choose

pink kisses for your lips, yellow
for your rare and glowing smile.
Stormy gray around your eyes
in the shape of furrowed earth—
like your father whose sole insufficiency
is a total lack of lighthearted childlikeness.
I would capture your superior
glare at the grocery store greeter
who says, Must need a nap, poor guy.

I would sculpt a thousand cracker crumbs
for you to pick up between two pinching fingers
and put in the carpet, to enjoy later.
I'd ring your mouth with stolen chocolate
and surround you with the clean kitchen towels
you pulled, unfolding so carefully, from the basket.

I lay your head against my shoulder,
your eyes closed, your breathing slow and soft
and fragrant as a fleeting lilac, so quick to bloom
and fade with summer's heat. I'd blow my prayers
as bubbles plashing in your clapping palms.

If I could paint a picture that would keep you
forever, I'd put it on the floor
and let you make it over
with knees and chubby hands,
laughing, laughing, those feet that stomp
the bathwater all across the rug
until you, yes you,
make a painting
of yourself.

Roar! 2018

Dreams of Night, c. 2003

Postpartum Preeclampsia

Nothing should be able to divert me from the curve
of his ear, the roundness of his tiny cheek.
Every moment should be spent wondering
how I could have been complete without you, a
mere
what was it, six days ago?

Should—A word far larger than its letters.
It hovers over days, nights,
tightens my jaw, works into my gut
until a bleakness swells and overshadows,
crushes inward like walls.

I am not well.

My attention drifts like the snow
collecting in corners of the porch
my mind
is absorbed by the puffiness
in my fingers, ankles,
the pain in my head,
numbers creeping higher: blood pressure,
proteins, messages left for the OB.

I know what could be,
what should not be—
motherless. Myself taken
from him, from myself.

I should enjoy these moments
while I am still here.

Dear, Dear Daughter (for Maggie)

I watch her when she doesn't know I'm looking,
in the family room, and think of how lovely she is
with afternoon sunlight painting
the curve of her cheek,
how kind, how overflowing
with talent as she dips a paintbrush in ocean blue
and sweeps it with grace and confidence across her page.

She leans close, frowning slightly, insisting
always that each mark is exactly perfect. I love
the stray marks, the blobs of color where she's testing
a new pallet, hesitant, unsure. She stands at the edge
of the future, not knowing how easily her limbs, strong now,
will carry her through the water.

I fear if I reach out my hand
she will push it away, saying
the weight of it is too heavy.

I fear if I reach out my hand
the weight of it
will hold her back.

Those Boots

Floating Child (for Kilian)

My son took hold of a balloon
one day, and floated up, up, up,
into the sky, laughing
he rose toward the trees,
above them, entirely
unconcerned, and so was I, not
worried in the least, not until
his round balloon and giggling feet disappeared
over rooftops.

My husband said, "He'll be fine,
he'll be back soon." So I thought nothing
of it until dinner. At my panicked insistence,
we drove around neighborhoods
to search.

What if his balloon had landed
and someone found him
and kept him? What if it dropped him
in a swimming pool? He was only
four, he couldn't swim. What if he let go?
I pressed my face to the window
as dusk faded and streetlights flickered on
one by one.
I looked out at trees glowing gold
in lamplight.

Two pale arms.
I shrieked, "Turn around! Turn the car around!"
And there he was, sitting atop the tree,
so small, baffled
by all this fuss.
I found a ladder,
climbed to the green carpet of leaves,
and held him

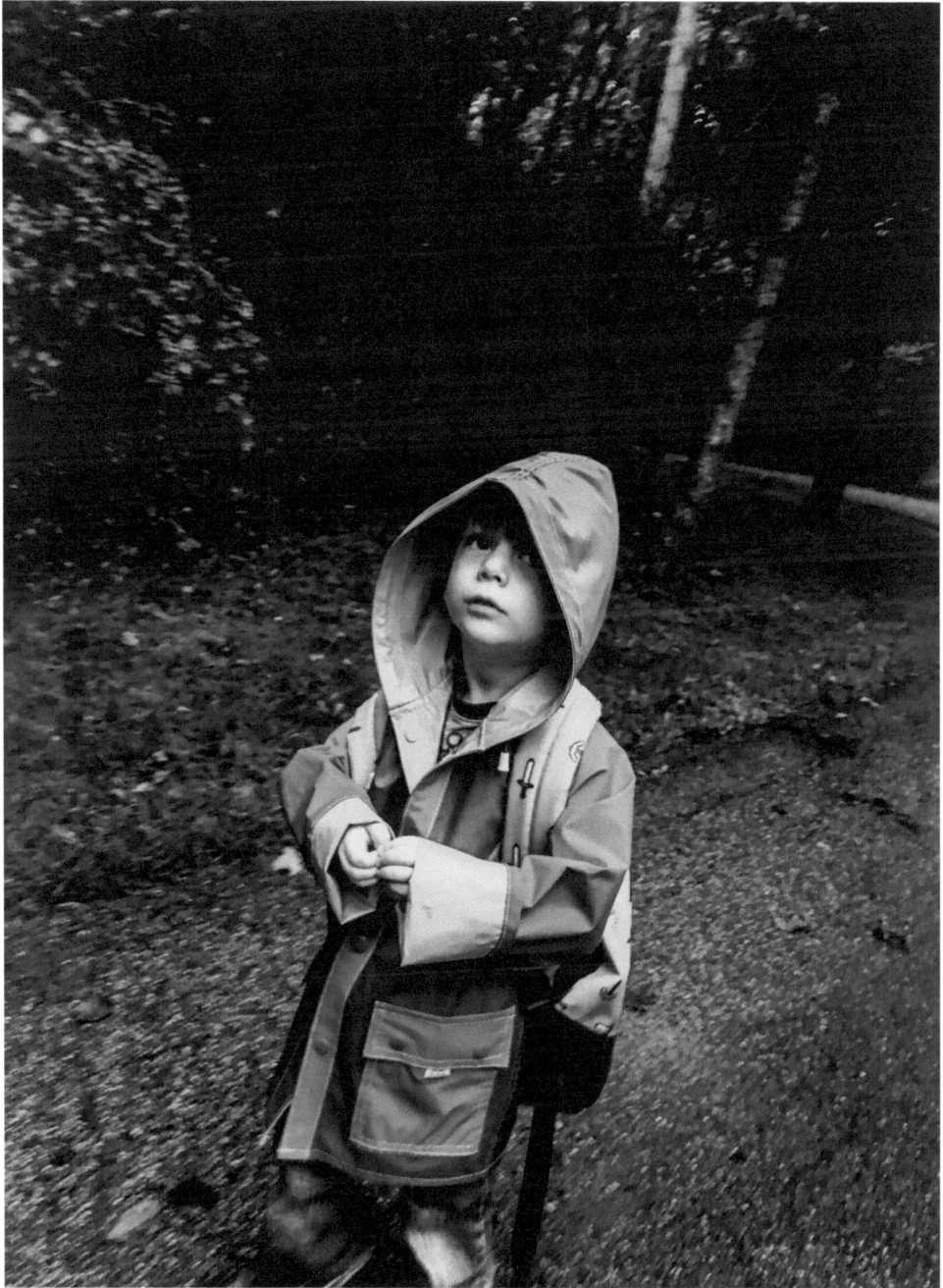

Where? 2019

the whole of that day,
the next,
each moment
as he eats his slice of pizza,
pages through a book,
my child with no words,
my child with a question mark above
his future like a party
balloon, I remember
my dream, and smooth his hair
lest any stray string catch on him
and carry him away.

[Substitutions]

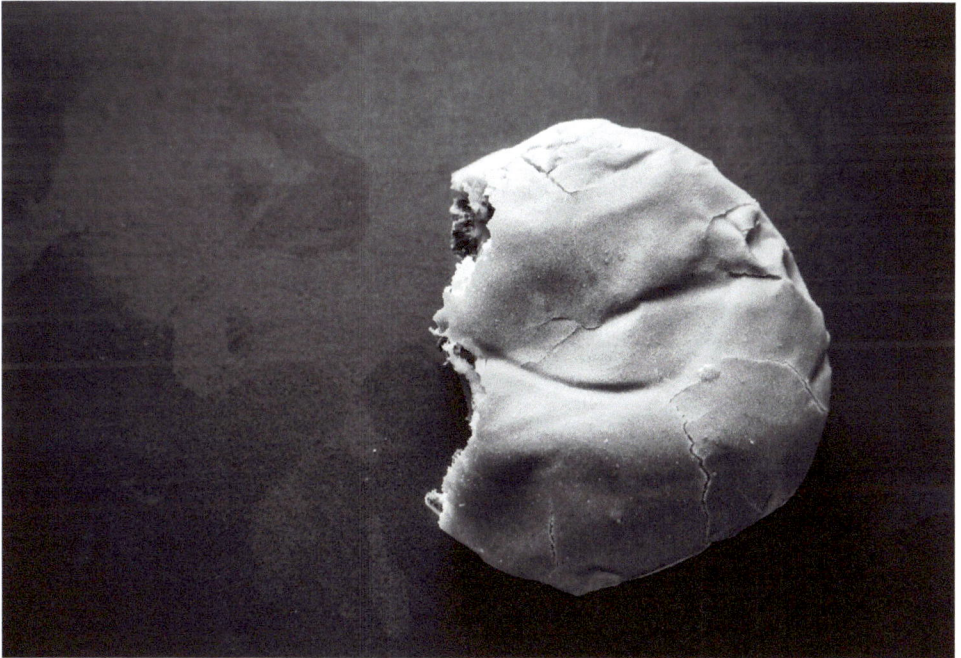

Bitten but not Consumed, 2011

McShame

I avoid refined sugars
in my home, the woman says.
We're at the library, children
playing in a plastic cottage, pretending
their mothers aren't sizing up
each child's kindness,
the eloquence
of their demands,
their own mothers'
fashion sense
and bony fingers.

(Only later did I think of Gretel's witch
her house the diabetic's nemesis.)
The woman says she cans organic,
and raises goats (for fertilizer
and milk for soap),
she breastfeeds
toddlers.
Other peoples'
toddlers? I ask,
No, just her own
in this unsweetened cage
before she eats them.

I think of her guiltily
as I ask my daughter what she'd like
for lunch,
hoping she'll want
nuggets and fries
that never decompose
so I can embalm myself with
Diet Coke and someday
we will both be immortal.

Shingles

Shingles are things on
the roof. They don't
itch or cause lasting pain.
They're not some childhood
virus reawakened by the stress
of being all grown up but still
child to someone.

They hurt. They pound into
your flesh like nails
and when you scratch them
they don't fall off, like curling
roof tiles my parents really should
have replaced long ago.
They just itch more.

Self, charcoal and pencil, c. 1997

Blood Sacrifice

*I*t had been years since she'd seen them,
blocked as she was on every social site because of that one time …
when I arranged a coffee date online, and she and he showed up.
People change, absence makes the heart

stupid and forgetful. I told her I had no photos
because it's the digital age, but she could take some
when we got together.

Together we walk
and every few steps she insists we stop.
She lifts her camera,
greedily, hungrily,
with each press of the shutter
devouring my children.

It does not quite sate her, I don't think,
because one child, uncomfortable
by this almost-stranger tasting tiny bits of her,
frowns for the camera.

While my daughter bounces ahead
I serve my mother an offering of words:
That girl, she's a challenge,
and more, a full platter of perfectly appetizing
insults against my own truth-seeing child.
All so my mother can take home
a satisfying lie.

The Burning, 2008

The Whoop-dee-doo Review ~ a Sonnet

At four my mother put our names inside
our snow pants, and a contest that I won.
A trip for four to Disney world—a ride
in coach, hotel, a three-night stay, and on
my pillow, mints. A tourist bus drove us
through dark and rain to entertainment called
the Whoop-dee-doo Review. Asparagus
and alcohol, my father's face grown red,
his laugh enough to draw the dancer down,
my mother's turn to pink up to her ears,
as long-limbed, limber girl, despite Mom's frown,
swung legs across Dad's lap. He laughed with tears
and slurring cheers. I'd seen this look and heard
that laugh and knew … Mom wouldn't say a word.

I rode my tricycle

I rode my tricycle on the open basement floor
the winter I turned four. Mom once painted
the concrete red with black splatters
and white dots, like a mime
in a pool of blood.

That was before Dad started keeping
every newspaper, magazine, broken
toaster, other people's broken toasters
until the floor was a strip, between tottering stacks,
of mime guts, worn away to concrete.

Mom screaming, Take your junk downstairs!
The vicious flurry of papers
flung against the wall, backhanded slaps,
Don't touch my stuff! that piled around our feet
like a reality television show we can't un-watch.

I take photos in 2009 from doorways.
Basement, kitchen, my old room.
The paths alone are two inches deep
and the toilet sits level with tissue wads
around a trash can, maybe, somewhere below.

I ask my mother when his hoarding started.
It was his mother, she said and flicked ants
off her water glass. She cleaned his room
with a garbage bag. Comic books.
We'd be millionaires if she hadn't
thrown it all away.

Before Selfies, c 1985

A Frayed Knot

I'm not sure when it happened, I mean, take out
the holes in memory filled with shadows where the map
declares here be dragons, and I had a happy childhood.
The memories I do have consist of visiting Christmas gifts
she put on layaway at Kmart, painting magnets with her
at the kitchen table, eating chicken noodle soup she heated
during one of my many, many bouts with strep throat,
and long days at home from school stitching, her helping me
thread a needle with moistened yarn over and over. I mean,
this woman nourished me from her own body, weaning me
only when her mother took ill after a stroke. I've nursed
my own babies, I know that tender, selfless act. I don't know
when it happened, when it broke or started breaking,
as if she was tied tightly with a fragile thread, fraying
after the loss of her mother, but she took the ends of string
and wrapped them around my tiny baby foot.
I'm sure I strained the thread, gradually, perhaps picking
at each strand, weakening them, and as a teen I pulled hard
until she, at last, began like an old sweater to unwind.

Then I had to wake her
before I left for school, entice her
out of bed by saying, *Breakfast*
and Burger King and I'll pay.
If I didn't
and often I didn't,
I'd wake her
when I came home,
afternoon sun glistening
across her unwashed hair.

It hurt
to pull the string,
it hurt more
to leave it,
wrapped so tight
I couldn't breathe.
My baby foot couldn't kick free,
and she needed, I mean,
I've nursed my own babies, I know
the closing of a tiny hand around
one finger
like it never, ever wants
to let go.

But it does. It wants to, needs to let go.
It hurts.... to cut the string.
I thought by now, surely, she had knotted
her own frayed ends.

One day I said, *Mother, I*—
Thank God! she cried,
and tossed a spit-moistened strand,
pulled it tight
around my neck,
as if somehow
with my own veins,
I can stitch her back together.

I Find Myself Here

Elusive Happiness

I touched her round cheeks.
Mama, you're so beautiful.
I climbed into her ample lap.
I like you this way,
you're soft.
But she was never happy.

Shopping makes her happy.
Dinners out make her happy.
Cake and ice cream for my child's
birthday make her happy.

My happiness
leaves her unmoved.
But my rejected manuscripts
make her happy.

I share my turkey dinners,
my Friday pizza nights,
my children's every special
moment of joy
with her. I refrain
from success,
pack my dreams
and nightmares
into a box.
So she might
be happy.

Coffee

I can't stop shivering
in this damned frigid
life, even with my favorite yellow
mug steaming between my palms.

I've nuked this cup
so many times it's dried
and cracking like the mud
on eleven random shoes

by the side door. It wasn't raining
when I got up this morning
but even the yellowing leaves
have decided it's time

to give up. The sky matches the beds
of my fingernails. It's ghastly,
that color, like I'm already
a corpse, and here I am, too cold

to bump up the thermostat,
clutching an empty mug, I should
give it up. Instead, I shiver all the way
back to the kitchen for a fresh cup.

Iced Coffee, 2019

I Miss My Mother

I shouldn't
she's still alive
and well, in a little
candy house.

I miss the idea.
Of a voice on the phone
to congratulate
without bemoaning her own
fading. Arms to enclose
without asking
if I have anything
to nibble.

I miss
Mother.
I always have.

[Preparation]

Finding the Way Through

UnInspiration

The baby babbling in his crib.
A teen cursing at the computer
screen and another two
bickering about whatever,
and Daniel Tiger singing about his potty
on repeat
like some demon-possessed music box
that never winds down.

The task I set myself is too hard.
It will take too much time.
I'm tired of it. Tired
in general. Tired of eating
vegetables. Tired of drinking water.

I want wine. I want an hour,
two hours, three, with no one
talking, no music playing,
not even the rooster crowing,
and I like the rooster's hoarse,
pathetic excuse of a crow.

I want someone to tell me
what I should do next
just this once. So my mind can rest
for two consecutive seconds. I tap the link
at the top of the page that says Done,
knowing it will never be true.

Flights on Wings of Steel

My not-tired eyes scan my bedroom's sloping ceiling,
dying air fern on my shelf, collection of porcelain dolls
balanced on lace handkerchiefs, and I inhale
the lingering scents of father's beer breath, unwashed armpit,
and closer, fresher scents of hot summer air baked by a day of sun.
Floating in the window is cooling mist
from the neighbor's sprinkler and sounds …
Outside the sun is fading
and I'm thinking how unfair it is
to be in bed
while Daddy watches television and basketballs pound pavement
in the street.

With the mourning dove's weeping, I hear it, a rhythmic tapping, clicking.
The sound flies out the downstairs window, tiny metal wings
to ricochet willy-nilly off the neighbor's drab brown house,
up to my window, my ears and beyond,
to chirp in the treetops. The birds tell stories
about talking flowers, secrets hidden
beneath a house along a bluff that's slipping, slipping
toward the bitter waters of Lake Michigan.
My mother plants a trunk of gold beneath that house
so when the lake takes the bluff and the house finally crumbles …

She's flying away on wings of typewriter keys.
When I tiptoe down the stairs for a last drink of water,
and I peek in to see Dad, eyes rheumy, open beer beside him,
I feel the clicking, clacking, clicking of her wingbeats
fanning my hot face.

I wonder, much, much later—
when my own fingers dance across my keyboard
into another world—
if perhaps that leaving
gave her strength enough
to stay.

Life History of My Pants

*M*y daughter and I shop at Goodwill
where she fits into everything she tosses on.
Standing in a dressing room of my own,
because she doesn't need to be comfortable
with my body, I stuff my deflated belly
into cargo pants I don't even like
because, pockets,
and fight, straining against
the fabric, to fasten the button,
and fail. Instantly the TV in my brain
starts playing all the reruns like some demented
Brady Bunch.
It was the story, of a woman named
Mommy, who couldn't keep from telling me …

It's a record with the needle stuck in the groove—
You're so lucky that you kept your red hair, mine faded,
no, you stole it—when you were born—
of my childhood.
You're so lucky you can fit into anything.
The Holy Mantra of the two of us crammed awkwardly into a single
dressing room at Goodwill, where I pretended I was comfortable
enough with my teenage body not to be embarrassed
by hers. She drew attention to it, Look at my belly,
I can't even button these pants, I hate this belly.
And she squeezed it, slapped it while telling me
over and over for so many years that I lost …
count. You're so lucky…
your husband supports you (mine doesn't)
your mother-in-law likes you (mine didn't)
your newborn son doesn't have colic as bad as your brother did,
I used to sit in the rocking chair
and cry right along with him.

I scramble desperately for the remote, punch
mute with a fist against my teeth.
I hang the pants
that rejected me on the rack
and I bite back words
that taste almost familiar.
I smile at her, my daughter,
talented, lovely, a delight like I imagine
I may have been,
perhaps, if I hadn't
been so damn lucky.

Outside the store I stop, inhale.
I mute the rerun again,
as many times as it takes.
Because I'm not lucky.
I'm freaking hashtag blessed.

Noise Canceling

The music playing on my headphones
is better suited for an episode of Star Trek,
one of those holodeck
adventures where the whole cast
hangs out in a jazz bar
pretending they're detectives while the ship
burns all to hell.
I'm at my holo-desk,
a fat dollop of peach
yogurt landing on my keyboard
and an uncapped marker leaving its signature
all down my sleeve. But the music
plays on. I bump up the volume
for the sax solo, sink
into the view outside the window
that is writing itself into a scene—

winter snow, marred only
by the footprints
of a solitary deer.

Paralysis

*I*f her character
goes to the Berkshires
a place I've never been
but seems like a place
people in books should go
and her husband dies
in a car crash just like
her mother years ago
then she will …
but if she goes
to the bank where
the robbers are just then
opening the vault …
or she takes a cab

instead of driving
and the cabbie is
insane and collects

human skin to make
his own jacket except
she is even more insane
and keeps him prisoner
until he writes her a novel …
Oh, what to do?
When you have thirty-seven minutes
before the baby wakes, and the
power
of all—of 78 unrestrained keys—
What do you do?

Wine & Rejection

MFA Writing Workshop

*J*ust because I bring a picture book
with princesses
and tattered holes in plot
from my daughter wearing that sparkly dress
every day for months on end,
you, fellow writers, cough into your morning coffees, suppress
laughter and yawns because
princesses, am I right?

I usually choose my best for writing workshop.
White linen, embroidered, the sort of frock
you'd never read around real children. But this once …
I thought I'd feign humility.
It looks good, plus it's,
you know, a work
in progress. Because,
workshop?

You assume I know nothing. I say,
as we discuss the other works,
Let your words carry your energy, let go
of the pow! of punctuation,
and you step in to translate,
for the benefit of all,
that dialogue tags and adverbs—the crutches of hacks
(like me?) ought be avoided.

I should have left my princess
at home with the costumes and glitter
that will never fully escape my living room carpet. How dare I
challenge you to think
about something so worthy
of sneers as the love of a mother
for her daughter's loves.
This book, a gift for her, I will tuck away
because of you.
I will save it
for my real life.

When He Was Always (for Baz)

Hey Mom? If we had a baby polar bear would we keep it
in the freezer? Hey Mom? If you had on a meat vest
and saw a pack of wild dogs and ran away
would they chase you? Hey Mom? What if you dropped
a potion in a cemetery and all the people
came up out of the ground as zombies? Hey Mom? Mama?
Mom? Wouldn't it be cool if gravity didn't exist?
Hey Mom? Where do homeless people go to hang out?
Hey, hey Mom? Did Clifford get so big from radiation?
Or from steroids? Mom, Mama? Who invented paper? Was it
the Egyptians? Or the Romans or the Greeks, no not them,
they invented wrestling. Hey Mama? Mom, do you really
sneak vegetables in our food? Mom? Hey Mom? Why
don't all the armies of all the countries in the world come together
to kill the zombies? Hey Mom? Do really rich people live
in Mentions? Mama, hey Mama, what's the lowest paying job?
Is the owner the highest or the lowest? What about
a pirate? Mom, if you had a secret hideout
that was underground and secret
where would you put the trap door? And you can't say,
in the bottom of the ocean. Mom? Hey Mom?
Are some costumes so scary that the people give them
all the candy? Mom! Hey Mom! What are you writing down?
Are you gonna post this online?

Eight years later I have my own questions
like, "What will the world do to
contain you?" He crouches in front of his laptop
that's taken up residence on the family room floor
and clicks his mouse, kicks off his heels and rolls
on carpet, crying in laughter at some meme.

His buddies chortle in their strange teen language,
Dude! That was sick! (Which doesn't mean, you know, actually
ill.) I watch how the years are shaping the sardonic arch
of his brow, and I wonder again, "What could the world
possibly do to contain him?"
I know only one thing
for certain. It will try,
and it will surely fail.

Unstoppable 2016

On Revision, Parenting, & Home Improvement

I drop a float-load of grout
on the glistening blue kitchen tiles.
I spread it with the cursor,
obscuring my perfect lines
into a flutter of color-coded note cards,
and books about saving cats
and elements of style like toddlers
who trim their own hair and sometimes
truly do need a time out in their room.

Painfully, I work
the grout into every joint, every crack,
and I hold the float at just the right angle
to pack a plot hole, and push down hard
(but not too hard)
to wedge a foot in a too-small
boot in hopes we can get one more
winter in this outdated kitchen.

The tiles are filmy, grainy still.
So I wipe tenderly, caressing
each word. Stripping the text of excess
quietly loudly smoothly hasteningly
as if anyone uses hasteningly,
and wiping away tears of classmate tauntings,
first heartbreaks, failures like knives in the cutlery drawer
until almost-adults smile for their senior
editor, ready to greet the delicious world.

[Serving Suggestions]

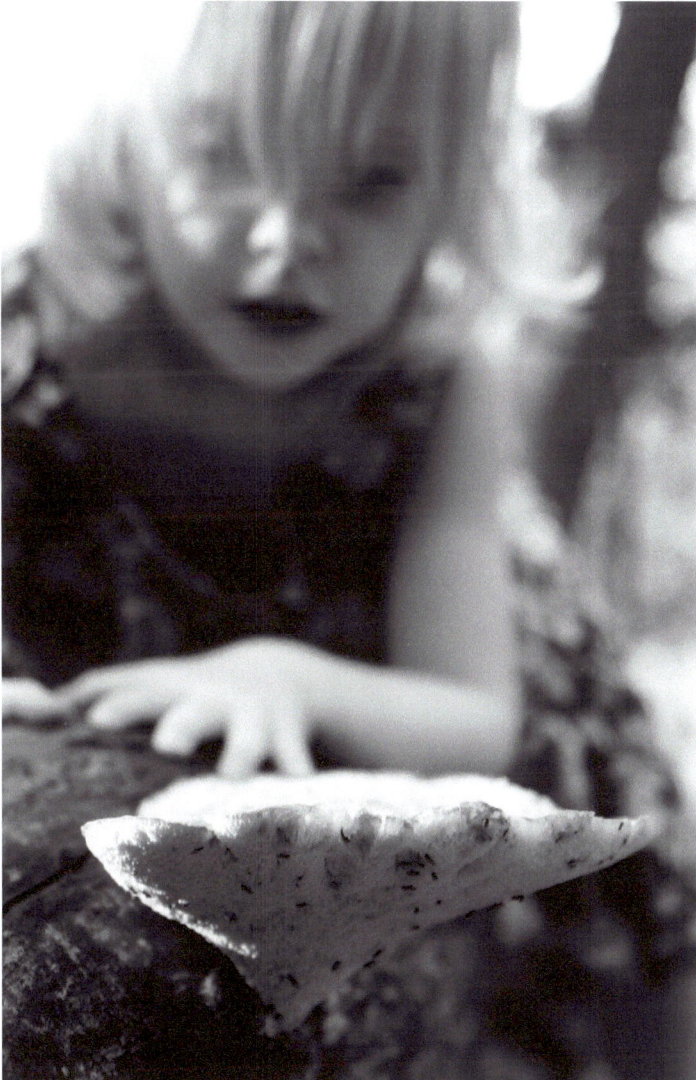

Wonder, 2008

Children of the Contemplative Spirit

Those round-eyed, bespeckled, tidy things
my husband and I once

imagined would read quietly in nooks, play
chess, by god, and the violin, and call a sweet

Yes, Mum, to a woman who does not exist.
I have spawned some other

breed. The sort who suck
the cat's tail to a fine point and paint

the baby a beard and unibrow
with sharpie, who battle

to the digital death with wars broken
into a thousand shards of concentration.

I'm not sure who breeds
the quiet, bookish children.

Certainly not the woman who sometimes
pulls that creepy doll from the closet

the doll with red ringlets and evil green eyes, and props her
right outside an unsuspecting child's bedroom door.

Questionable Alliances

Guess She's Not a Dancer (for Penny)

I watch you, daughter, skip across the floor,
dancing your fuchsia self on purple-striped legs
from one studio mirror to the next while
the other half-sized ballerinas prance in perfect
black and pink, toes pointed, teacher cooing,
"What pretty feet!" With you she grimaced,
I think having given up on any hope for your feet.
But you didn't notice, I hope. You certainly
don't seem troubled as you pull faces in the mirror
and whip your nearest classmates with your ponytail.

I catch all of this in a video, share online,
guiltily, with the wry caption, You'll never guess
which little dancer is mine! :-/

You're not first in our family to be given up as lost.
Your oldest brother's preschool parent-teacher conference
went something like, He doesn't seem to
listen or use play equipment quite the way
the other children do. I had laughed, picturing the racetrack
for his Matchbox cars arranged in orange arcs on the couch,
I make sculpture! he said. I recall in detail
the lines of the teacher's mouth, puckered, frowning
when I told her that he sang every song just fine
for me at home.

I scan the comments on my post.
❤ ❤ ❤ ❤
My girl was just like her! and other such
commiserations. Plus the one comment
that stays with me still, the one that pulls me
back to your good-morning embrace, holding, holding
holding you until you determine it's time to bounce on
your pretty feet, the ones you didn't share
in class, to other worlds of excitement.

I know which child is yours, one friend said.
The joyful one, of course!

Before the Show, 2019

What Publishing Will Do For You

I read an essay once
by some writer (okay, Anne Lamott),
who likened publishing to the soaring eagle
on a credit card that only seems

to fly.
What would she know?
She's published.

But so am I, finally, and I can agree.
Row upon row upon row
of shiny spines
beneath little bulbs
like celebrity spotlights
on tracks along the ceiling
are nothing

compared to a cookie crumb
between pages
of your latest manuscript
because he just couldn't wait
until you were done writing
to find out
what came next.

Fashion Statement

*M*y son is wearing his shirt
backward. I don't notice
until noon, when he's at the table
poring over a library find
about amazing and disgusting
strange, bizarre real-life
feats. A man who can pass
a snake in his nose and out
his mouth, or a woman who
can fit herself in a bottle,
eat her way out of ten
thousand worms. You know,
fascinating stuff, so much more
important than putting
the tag in the back.

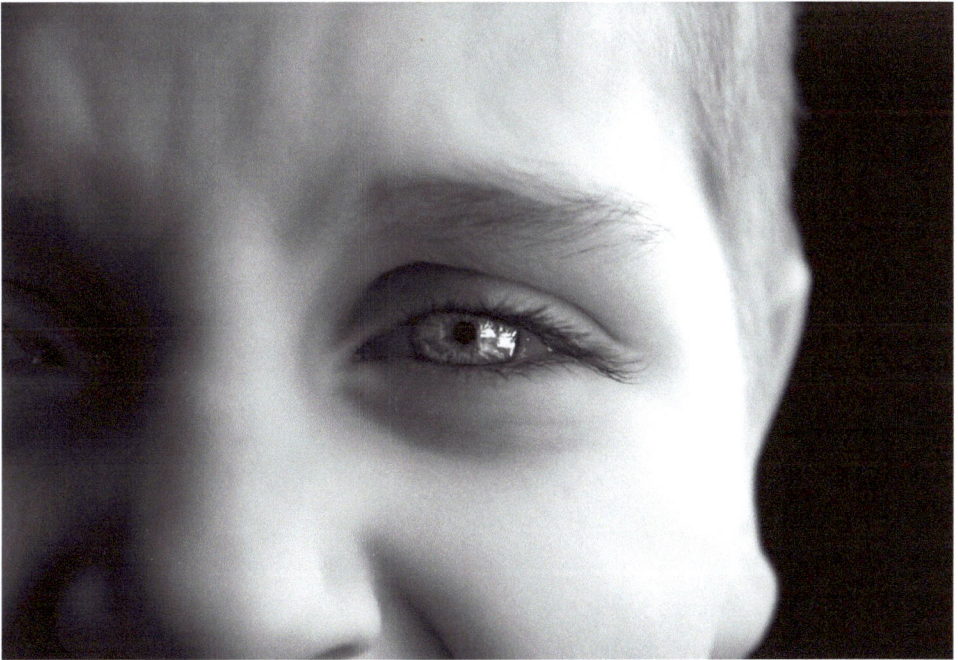

Eyes, 2007

Son in the Night (for Nicholas)

*L*ast night my son wept into his hands. His
long fingers caught tears and held them
like wishes, his childhood dripping in a stream
of snot from the tip of his nose. He's a man now.

Legally he has been one for several months, he shaves
daily thanks to hairy genes from his father, and the top
of my embrace brushes his chin. Except last night. He
sat in the chair, elbows on knees, hands clutching ragged hair.

I cradled his head in the crook of my arm, as I did
that first morning after ninety excruciating minutes of bearing down.
He has outgrown me, as I kneel beside him, his broad shoulders
shaking, his sobs the only sound in the perfect gloom.

When he was only four I awakened to a thud and found him
beside his bed, still asleep, his forehead bruised by the little red
table, legs shaped like pencils. I gathered him up and tucked
Bob the Builder sheets under his chin, murmured kisses into his hair.

My words would be shadows too indistinct for him to see.
He's a man now. Magic-Mama kisses, bandaids, my arms
are no longer strong enough. I inhale the fragrance of his hair,
unchanged by years, and I pray silently that his way forward will be
beautiful.

The Way Forward, 2017

Woods

In the woods in the front yard
I carved out a sheltered spot
where the leaves meet
to form a roof and tree trunks bend
inward gently. The air
smells of blackberries.

I took my children there,
see this secret place
I made for you?
A hideout, a garden?

They went back inside
and turned on the television.

I return
and the mysterious wind
speaks to me
in a voice only I
can hear.

They will find
their own way
it says
when you are not watching.

Yesterday's Song

Keep on lovin'
fades into rap
and I tap my foot
in time to Baby's
hiccups. The school bus is late
so it's my fate to jam in the minivan
like the approaching-mid-aged
I-hope-not-soccer mom I fear—
I am
until the radio reaches the ten minute
silence to preserve battery life
and the crunch of gravel
becomes music
of a yellow school bus blurring
in the mirror of tomorrow
is closer than it appears.

Discovery, 2019

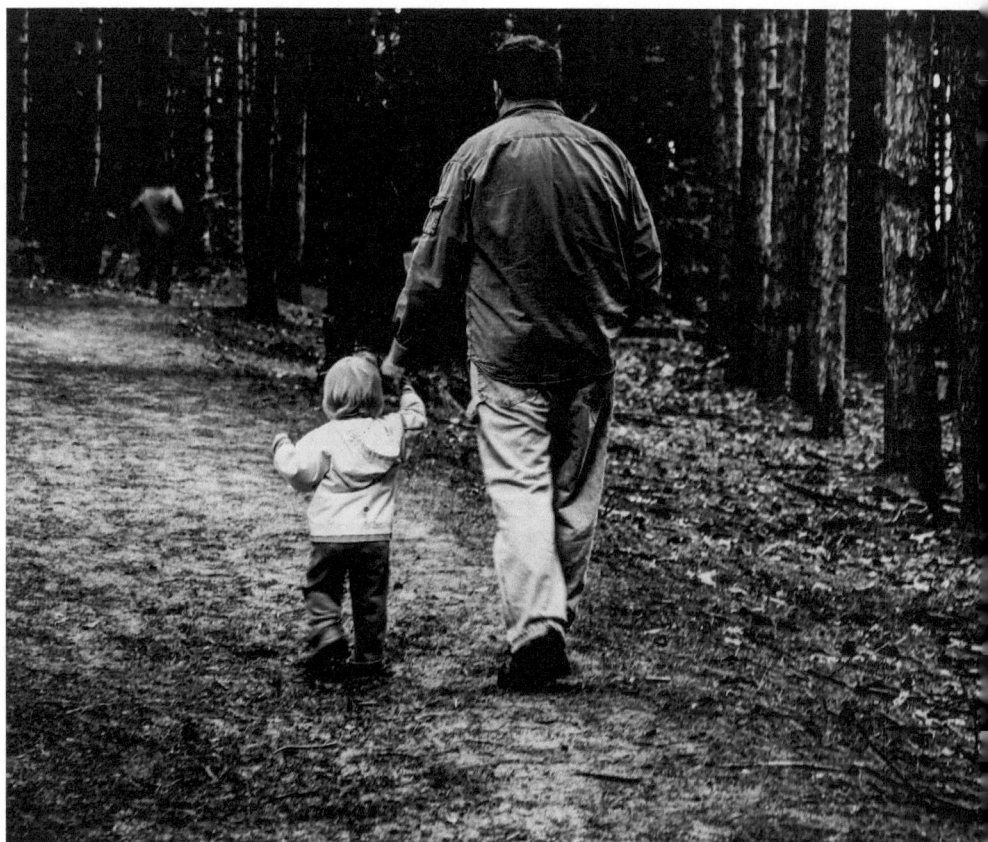

Walk in the woods, 2007

Anniversary

I should write a poem
of love to my husband
of more than twenty years today.
I've lost track of the number
of evening glasses of wine, conversations
about who will change the baby, months—no, years—
of nightly awakenings for him to stumble past me
into baby's room, pick him (or her) up and neatly roll
him to my midnight breast. All those nights have merged
into one, long dozing hour in the glider, feet up, hubby
snoring softly from his side of the bed while mine
grows cool. Twenty-something years of conversations
about vasectomies, what to make for dinner that will by some miracle
please everyone. Twenty-ish years of trimming less and less
of his hair, of holding his arm in bed and whispering stories
of the day and prayers for tomorrow.

Twenty … Ah, it's too much math, let our son figure it out,
the one who asked, "When did you and Dad have sex
to make the baby?" And more than twenty years of that, half those years
in therapy to right the wrongness of all the years before,
and a quarter of them (see, fractions!) with breath held,
the future unknown, our only certainty our togetherness.

And so we celebrate. Life is what it is.
He drove the teens to school, I
did algebra and practiced sounding out
the word L O V silent E.
We treated ourselves to dinner out
with the kids
and a coupon.

After Midnight

Sometime after midnight, Daddy gets one of them feral cats in his sights
 and bang, he shoots it dead.

Around 3am, Mama says I've read quite enough, so I better switch
 off my light. I do, but switch it back on again as soon as
 she goes back downstairs.

At some late hour, I'm up to go potty. I forget to lift the
 lid. Mama yells for me to stop, but I make a waterfall
 all over the bathroom floor.

In the middle of the night, I catch a glimpse of Santa Claus.
 He's nothing but a red blur in the hall. I pee fast as I can, but when I
go looking,
 he's already gone. Mom and Dad say I was dreaming, but I know
 what I saw.

Around 3:16am, my nightlight burns out. I can't breathe
 in that kind of dark.

Just after midnight, Mom and Brother and I watch Daddy from the
window.
 He lights off leftover July Fourth firecrackers in the snow.
 It's New Year's Day.

Timeless rain becomes a metronome on our tent's thin roof.
I question the wisdom
    of camping on our honeymoon,
    and wonder what axe murderer
    or rabid creatures lurk in the wild Pennsylvania night.

Around 5am, I nurse my son in the rocking chair. A street light
    outside the window
    frosts his hair. I whisper a lullaby.

Around two in the morning, I conceive my daughter. My husband
    has a little something to do with it, too.

Around two or three, the whole house trembles. My husband
    lurches out of bed. We find our son sprawled on the rug
    in his room, still asleep.

Sometime in the night, I hear a creak on the stairs.
I cling to my husband's arm
    and try to go back to sleep.

Almost 6am, the power is out at our new house. My husband and I
    stand in the driveway. We listen to dawn wake the sleeping world.

Thirst

It swells along the lip,
trembling,
refusing to fall.
So I reach out my tongue
and nurse it,
that last sweet
drop of wine.

When the Children go to Bed

My love empties the dishwasher
every morning. Red Fiestaware nestles
with yellow, with royal purple
as I slide them behind doors
of finger-smudged glass.

The wine glasses clink
as he dries them. He stows
them in the cupboard
together in the dark
where they wait
for bedtime

beside sippy cups and a plastic bowl
with a cow
leaping the round, ripe
moon.

Portrait of a Man, c. 2014

What they find, 2008

planting season

I pierce earth with
the sharp point of my spade.
I cut out a little square
that I hope is about
the same size as the box
of dirt and roots and crayons
that I submerge
with vines tangled
in my hair and worms

crawling over the bridge
of my nose. I breathe
moist earth, ecstatic
as a mole in spring.

The Lord Honors

*B*e thankful to the Lord above
His steadfast love endures forever
He who makes chickens bob their heads
His steadfast love endures forever
And who causes soft blankets to soothe
restless infants
His steadfast love endures forever.
Be grateful, oh heart, for teenagers
His steadfast love endures forever
Though they rise up at night
to eat bagels or take showers
His steadfast love endures forever
Though they hack the password off your computer
and change your background to Grumpy Cat
His steadfast love endures forever
Thank the Lord your God for toddlers and preschoolers
His steadfast love endures forever
Though they discover old gumdrops beneath the couch
and eat them
His steadfast love endures forever
Though they always
seem to find the permanent markers
His steadfast love endures forever
Be grateful, oh heart, for socks
that clog the vacuum
His steadfast love endures forever
And the many feet
that track mud into your house
His steadfast love endures forever

The Lord honors pure and noble hearts
His steadfast love endures forever
He leads you through tears
of miscarriages, injury, loss
His steadfast love endures forever

He sits beside you in the dark of night
His steadfast love endures forever
When grief or rage seek to overtake you
His steadfast love endures forever
He comforts you with the sweetness
of a thank you,
the warmth of a winter fire
His steadfast love endures forever
He calls you back to him
with tiny fingers
wrapped around your thumb
His steadfast love endures forever
He welcomes you
with thudding tail and happy, clicking claws
His steadfast love endures forever

Go forward now, dear mother of children
His steadfast love endures forever
Do not fear this shadow-filled time when the path is obscure
His steadfast love endures forever
Know that he will guide you and will give you words when you have none
His steadfast love endures forever
Believe that he longs for good and truth and beauty
even more than you do
His steadfast love endures forever

For he is good and faithful, always
His steadfast love endures
Forever

The First Step

Design

The font selected for this book is Garamond Typeface. A Parisian printer, Claude Garamond, brought the first typeface of this kind about in the 16th century A.D. during the Renaissance period and at the beginning of his career for King Francis I. Best of all, it was based on the handwriting of the king's librarian, Angelo Vergecio. Robert Slimbach, working with Adobe, set about creating a new version of the Garamond font family in the late 1980s with its elegant antique feel, and not least, an eco-friendly type because it uses less ink. This book was designed by Kevin Callahan for the 2019 FountainVerse Poetry Festival in Kansas City
with cover art by Polly Alice McCann
and photography by the author.

Look out for more books by
FLYING KETCHUP PRESS

◦ kNew: The Screenplay — T.L. Sanders
◦ kNew: The Chapbook

◦ Road Map: Poems, Paintings & Stuff — Kēvin Callahan

◦ Kinlight: Homegrown Poems — Polly Alice McCann
◦ Tea with Alice: Heirloom Poems

◦ The Very Edge: Poems in English, Spanish & French — Various Authors

◦ Tales from the Dream Zone
◦ Tales from the Goldilocks Zone

◦ Melody Shore Mysteries — Carole Lynn Jones

FLYING KETCHUP PRESS to discover and develop new voices in poetry, drama, fiction and non-fiction with a special emphasis in new short stories. We are a publisher made by and for creatives in the Heartland. Our dream is to salvage lost treasure troves of written and illustrated work-- to create worlds of wonder and delight; to share stories. Maybe yours. Find us at www.flyingketchuppress.com

Rebecca Grabill

Sweetened Condensed is two parts sugar, three parts milk: the life of a writer and mother of six encapsulated into raw moments of lyrical free verse with the author's black and white photography. Rebecca Grabill's first collection brings her readers home to rural Michigan and into the world of a woman on the path less traveled-- wife, daughter, teacher, author, and mother of six. She writes, "I love words, the music they make, their personalities and scents and textures. Words are like Sendak's *Wild Things*, each clamoring for their own Rumpus. I love creating stories by taming a few of those wild and wily words, and I love inspiring others to explore their own creativity."

Rebecca is an award-winning author. She has an MFA in Writing for Children and Young Adults from Hamline University and is a Sustainable Arts Foundation awardee and is represented by Victoria Wells Arms of Wells Arms Literary and Karen Neumair of Credo Communications. She lives in rural Michigan with her husband, six children, and two cats.
Follow her at https://www.rebeccagrabill.com or on Facebook.

More Books by Rebecca Grabill

Halloween Good Night (Atheneum Books for Young Readers)
Violet and the Woof (HarperCollins)
A Year with Mama Earth (Eerdmans Books for Young Readers)

Rebecca's poetry and essays have appeared in Farm Magazine, SNReview, Parenting from the Heart, Asinine Poetry, Hip Mama, Medulla Review, Main Street Rag and more. She speaks regularly at Calvin University and is a Sustainable Arts Foundation Awardee.

Follow her online at www.rebeccagrabill.com
IG @rebeccawritesbooks
Twitter @rebeccagrabill

www.ingramcontent.com/pod-product-compliance
Lightning Source LLC
Chambersburg PA
CBHW041531090426
42738CB00036B/114

9 781970 151190